from The Mountain of California ...

from **The Mountain of California ...**

R.T.A. Parker

Openned Press
www.openned.com/press

First published in 2010 by Openned Press, London
www.openned.com/press

A CIP catalogue record for this book is available from the British Library.

ISBN-13: – 978-0-557-58775-9

JPD

[*who's in* | *each of* | *these pines.*]

INTRODUCTORY..1

I..3

1. BASEBALL 5
2. BART 6
3. NILES WITH THRUSH...7
4. PIER 39 8
5. DUMBARTON BRIDGE..9
6. MALLS 10
7. TRAIN TRAIN TRAIN 11
8. PONDEROSA 12
9. AQUATIC PARK 13
10. CALTRAIN...14
11. GARDENING..15
12. JACK CASADY..16

II..17

13. POWERSHOT A470 19
14. SUBURBS 20
15. COLUMNS..21
16. CONDOTTIERI 22
17. MARINE LAYER...23
18. CALIFORNIA BEAR 24
19. PACIFIC 25
20. COCA-COLA 26
21. WATER...27
22. BUG SCREEN..28

23. STARLEET ACADEMY....29
24. SEA OTTER....30

III....31

25. AIR....33
26. PACIFIC....34
27. THE STORM OF CONFUSION....35
28. MECHANICS OF PINECONE....36
29. HORSE & DOG : CONSTRUCTION OF MYTHOS....37
30. AMTRAK....38
31. CRICKET....39
32. SOIL....40
33. SAND....41
34. MUNI....42
35. LA....43
36. SEQUOIA....44

IV....45

37. MARIPOSA....47
38. MANN IN LA....48
39. MOUNT DIABLO....49
40. BIOGRAPHY....50
41. PARADISE....51
42. THESIS ENVOI....52
43. TIME....53
44. AQUATIC PARK....54
45. ICY RITTER....55
46. UN CAMINO DE NOCHES....56
47. LAG....57

48. PACIFIC 58

V. 59

49. SANTA CRUZ 61
50. APOLLO 62
51. SF ZOO 63
52. GHIRARDELLI'S : CHEEK 64
53. MARINE LAYER 65
54. NORTH BEACH 66
55. RED & WHITE LINES 67
56. JOHN MUIR 68
57. GOLDEN GATE 69
58. WAVE 70
59. A NEAR VIEW OF THE HIGH SIERRA 71
60. CHEMICAL TANK CAR 72

VI 73

61. HOPPER FOR GRAIN 75
62. FLIGHT 76
63. ROCKIES 77
64. BART 78
65. NILES — SUNOL 79
68. 2068 82
71. NILES CON HPV 85
72. CHEESEBURGER 86

VII 87

73. SNOW ON PINES 89

74. Dispersed Forest 90
75. Capitol Corridor Intercity Rail 91
76. Essanay Café 92
77. Lamp Fracas 93
78. 78 94
79. Bicycle 95
80. Eucalyptus 96
81. LAX 97
82. SFO 98
83. Catastrophe 99
84. Mornings 100

VIII 101

85. SFO 103
86. F Train 104
87. Production 105
88. Ikea 106
89. Lumber Yard 107
90. '49 108
91. Object-Pine 109
92. San Francisco Bay 110
93. Track 111
94. Limbo 112
95. Mission Peak Trails 113
96. Trails 114

IX 115

97. Bulbs 117
98. State 118

99. DREAM 119
100. GAOL IN SPAIN 120
101. PARK STATE 121
102. FRUITVALE...122
103. LAST BART TO RICHMOND 123
104. ENGLAND...124
105. THE GOLDEN STATE 125
106. PACIFIC 126
107. SKYNET CENTRAL 127
108. SKY 128

X 129

109. INSIGNIA 131
110. CALIFORNIA BEAR'S ORDEAL......................................132
111. WARTIME COURAGE 133
112. LIGHT & KNOWLEDGE 134
113. THE END 135
114. THE END 136
115. THE END 137
116. XTZBK49HT 138
117. PACIFIC...139
118. THE END...140
119. MUSIC...141
120. BALL..142

ENVOI 143

Acknowledgements

Versions of 'Introductory', 9, 10, 16, 27, 45, 49, 59, 63, 89, 90 & 91 have previously appeared in *Naked Punch*; 13, 15, 16 & 24 in *Wolf*; 44, 51, 54, 82, 95 & 102 in *Klatch*; 1-8, 11 & 12 in *Onedit*, 3 in *Column Space* & 37, 91 & 'Envoi' in *The Rialto*.

Datelines indicate date & location of first complete drafts. Much of Section I was written during sessions of the 2009 Sport & Literature Association Conference at the University of Western Ontario in London, Ontario, making use of various ideas & some language from the papers presented there. 1 was written with the SLA in mind, though it preceded that conference. 12 & 14 were written during sessions of the 2009 Ezra Pound International Conference in Rome, making use of various ideas & some language from the papers presented there. 12 quotes Alex Pestell. 14 was written during & quotes from Ron Bush's paper in Rome. 23 paraphrases Philip Whalen. 20, 29, 40, 46, 52, 71 & 78 quote materials from poems, translations & correspondence by Jessica Pujol Duran. 30, 31, 33 & 34 use materials from the BBC's Test Match Special broadcasts & websites, as well as other BBC sources. 30 includes lines taken from the conclusion of a review by J.H. Prynne of *The Pattern of Hardy's Poetry* by Samuel Hynes, *Victorian Studies* 5 (1961-62). 36 quotes Francesca Lisette. 41 quotes James Murdoch. 44's source text is *Paradise Lost*, Book I. 45, 55, 56, 59, 60, 61, 63 & 107 use extracts from a copy of John Muir's *The Mountains of California* given to me by Peter Nicholls. 47's source text is Doug Magee and Robert Newman's *All Aboard ABC*. Much of 48-58 were written during sessions of the 2009 New Clear Forms Conference at the University of Glasgow, making use of various ideas & some language from the papers presented there. 58 was written during & quotes from Ben Hickman's paper. 71's source text is 3, as translated into Spanish by Jessica Pujol Duran. 75 paraphrases Pablo Neruda, Queen, Ezra Pound, Robert Rehder, Simon Jarvis & Keston Sutherland. 77 approaches a poem by Abi Curtis. 91, 92 & 102 quote Journey's 'Lights'. 93-96 quote various dictionary definitions & paraphrase Martin Heidegger. 96 quotes Pound's *Jefferson and/or Mussolini*. 98's source text is Alexander Pope's *Iliad*, Book VII. 100's source text is an email from Dick Crepeau. 101 & 102's source texts are 44 & 98. 105 quotes Theodor W. Adorno's foreword to *Prisms*. 111 quotes a dedication written for Tom White by Gordon Brown in his *Wartime Courage*. 112's source text is this 'acknowledgements'. 114 quotes Van Wyck Brooks's *The Ordeal of Mark Twain*. 117 quotes Barbara Cartland. 119 contains part of a translation of Jack Spicer's 'For Jack'. 120's source text is 1. See 'An Index' for further details of quotations. I have forgotten & concealed other sources.

Introductory

SOW & | test the | full scale
Of Cal | iforn | ia
Seeds ; pine | nuts & | sperm

Of pine | cones that | under
Torrid | sun & | the sky
Blue that | turns as | spacemen

Adrift | cross night | sky
At the | mall with | fingers
Of comm | odi | ty thus

Our shared | gamut | runs from
Guard dog | chained at | Presid
Io | to turn | ing Bay.

6/x/9 – Abergavenny

I

1. Baseball

OH ROVER, | snow-flake | that snow
Flakes train | window with
Res'nant | cow | bell

For ket | tle corn. | That it
Might staunch | ily | staunch my
Leaking | heart if | you stood

At the | far left & | I'm at
Th'centre | of all | of it,
Roll on | Vespa | across

Out-field | onto | the grey
Square ac | cess ramp | of the
Oakland | Coli | seum.

17/vi/9 — Falmer

2. BART

OUR TRAIN | little | little
Train is | through with | the hills
Of Niles, | breaks cloud | canopy

To the | steamy | swollen
Inter | ior. O | little
Train reads | his L | CD

Of love | affairs | & men
Run-through, | broken, | raised up.
— If you | would like | to know,

I live | in the | lit pre
Diction. | It's all | future,
All this | coming | furrow.

23/vi/9 — London, Ontario

3. Niles With Thrush

Your hot | sands, your | blue up
Per layer ; | vineyard, | a
Goat | (which is a | précis).

Old Europe | her bidet,
Won't apply | in Fremont.
& Chinese / contra | ception

Through | deferral | like a
Forest | fire, that | will not
Apply | for Frémont. | His

Mexi | can a | percu.
In peace | time the | child takes
Credit | f'r its cess | ation.

25/vi/9 — London, Ontario

4. Pier 39

EACH WORD | makes an | other
Restrict | ion ; & | it is
So for | all sen | tences

That ass | ert.
So, in | the new | world, we
encour | age ex | pansion

Of ne | gations. | I did
Not choose | a bit | of shark
& a | piece of | swordfish

On rice. | Never | loved you
In any | sense. | Allow
Our past, | it[']s ex | pansiveness.

25/vi/9 – London, Ontario

5. Dumbarton Bridge

THE MOST | culti | vated
Ital | ian ten | or that
Ever | lived sang | on this

Dumbart | on Bridge,
His ex | igence | the roar
Of the | Ponde | rosas

Which is | concom | itant
To the | ubi | quitous
Stench of | fallen | needles

That haunts | these shores. | On the
Freeway | the pines | present
All pasts.

25/vi/9 — London, Ontario

6. Malls

Here you | can't say | a thing
That's not | resis | tance. Though
It is | more fit | ting here

To mourn | our just | lost youth
Just like | an in | crement
Your cap | itu | lation

Is a | complic | ity,
Death walks | the malls,
The | Coli | seum

& through | the fragrant | pines,
So rest | quiet, | & hear
Commod | ities' | maxim.

26/vi/9 – London, Ontario

7. Train train train

SHOVED HOT | rolls in | her mouth
For just | a second, | pleased with
What seemed | as if | it might

Be a | moral | question
Revealed | as a
Social | question, | it's done ;

Its æs | thetic | is mown
Excess | as spring's | green mow
In the | humid | inner,

Fullest | extent | is its
Creation | of coast | line
Collab | ora | tion, sand.

26/vi/9 – London, Ontario

8. Ponderosa

I ATE | my protein | pill
At Lake | Eliz | abeth —
In a | year & | a ½

I will | have been | Cap
Tain of | the 9, | head coach
Of the | 11 | &

Assistant | coach | of the
9 ; I | shall turn | agg
Ressor | & un | sex you

The hard | & gross | pine mulch
The pine | cone in | terjects
The seed | the sex | the fires.

27/vi/9 — London, Ontario

9. Aquatic Park

I love | you your | hover
Pack, one | thing in | the world.
In Cal | iforn | ia

It's so | boring, | perfect
Meta | phor no | longer
Meta | phor, just | like a

Perfect | pitch is | not quite
Any | pitch, or | new light
Out of | matte black | is

All of | the crap | removed
& that | that
Remains | simu | lates light.

27/vi/9 — London, Ontario

10. Caltrain

IT'S WHEN | you can't | decide —
Can't see | the æs | thetic,
I'm sorry, | can't see | the

Ethical ; | my
Love out | from that
Beach Boys | song

& other | ephem | eral
Shit that
I

Think a | bout, these | stupid
Things, their | diaph | anous
Partic | ulars | binding.

27/vi/9 — London, Ontario

11. Gardening

THEIR SPEECH | equates | with death,
This green | noisy | island.
Their eq | uanim | ity

In chall | enge of | curves on
The reg | istra | tion desk,
Our pan | galax | ial

Curved reg | istra | tion desk.
So your | bright charged | moments,
Musk a | bashes | &

Ever | negates, | discourse
Apes | complex | mechanics
[Not na | ture] of | pine cone.

28/vi/9 — London, Ontario

12. Jack Casady

AH SUN | blush, you | cherry,
Incon | stant cann | ibal
That cor | responds | to

The the | ory of | corres
Ponden | ces, in | coher
Ance, so | called world, | salad.

I should | egg your | pudding,
Prelim | ina | ry spud,
Dispatch | the medi | nuns

They've been | in transit | for
58½
Hours, so | pungent, | growing.

1/vii/9 – Rome

II

13. PowerShot A470

IS UN | HEIMLICH | in its
Multi | ple re | fusal
Of imm | anence. | Christ's first

Technol | ogy | burned out
At Vi | aregg | io ;
Toge | ther con | front time,

Self, au | thori | ty of
Postcard | vendor, | thingness,
Process, | repro | duction :

If … it | would say … : | 'all speech
Discon | tinues | & is
Being's | dissem | inate.'

5/vii/9 – Sienna

14. Suburbs

for Ron Bush

POTENT | IAL | ITY
OF light's | veer from | over
Tiered pa | rasol | as nail

In plank | retains | its steel
Integ | rity | & is
In truth | as one | with it,

Though no | right-think | er would
Broach this | funda | mental.
The peg's | integ | rity's

Tag | extern | al as
Sheath of | wall. Which | is hell.
Illus | 'ry & | sep'rate.

2/vii/9 – Rome

15. Columns

WHEN POUND | & a | Williams
In Ve | rona | their column
They did | not con | sider

The strip | mall, which | is
Endless | & bar | oque ; its
Irre | voca | ble &

Ubiq | uitous | thingness
A sem | inar | on
Dassein, | the green | marble

Its in | terchange | able
Pillar | portage | passport
To the | corporate | nation.

6/vii/9 — Florence

16. Condottieri

OUR DI | ASPORA | in
Cali | forni | a found
In the | distended | small

City | states of | Staples
& Geico | & Michaels
About | which wind | the vines,

Arbours, | begar | landed
Grottos | of ro | coco
Thingful | ness that | are in

The hot | tarmac | & the
Cold, the | blown dry | leaves of
Wrath-con | scious cap | ital.

6/vii/9 – Florence

17. Marine Layer

A VOICE | & no | thing more
Difficult | to under | stand
Than the | passion | ate

Seldom | safe in
Their own | hearts, let | alone
In their | rela | tions with

Others, | a | new kind
Of a-novel | our | passion
Ate through. | Such as, | she says,

Ador | no on | A. Rod
Opera / | object | on the /
A path | that brooks | no turn.

7/vii/9 – Paris

18. California Bear

CREEP CAL | IFORN | IA
Bear, to | Jessi | ca P.,
& with | your bones | whisper

My part | ial | ity.
To her | Sienese | twirl,
In sec | lusion | pretty

Toes, up | campa | nile
A high | cleanly | bird-cheap
木 | side-swept | unfurls

Into | a faulty | sleep.
A hi | bernate | heavier,
Cali | fornia | bear creeps.

19/vii/9 — Falmer

19. Pacific

BLOW NOW | loud thou | unpeace
Ful sea, | subdue | troubled
Teenag | ers, to | whom sea

Extends | quiv'ring | pity,
Pretty | ocean | endless
Without | horiz | on on

Every | *single* | one of
Its sides, | within | which all
Viol | ence is | concen

Trated. | Iso | late grey
Nightmare, | you kind | & time
Generous | paci | fic joy.

19/vii/9 – Falmer

20. Coca-Cola

RED SOFT | rose I | saw a
Bloody | mermaid | with a
Rocket | pack. Your | secrets

Are as | your bond | bound up
So that | maybe | I'll make
You a | mix-tape | while your

Secret's | piney | rose star
Pines for | him out | from out
Over | Zara | goza

In which | secrets | abound,
& you | like a | Coca-
Cola | without | a sound.

20/vii/9 — Falmer

21. Water

YOU ARE | water | & I
Pine for | your pine | kiss, touch
Of rose | petals | sand dry ;

The wet | sand, the | dry mulch
Of Cal | iforn | ia —
Resin- | baptised, | enough

Woman | & thorn | ier
To shock | roses | with shine
[Under | standing | weather],

Our pac | ific | decline.
JP | D straight | high [in]
Constant | fragrant | dark pine.

20/vii/9 — Brighton

22. Bug Screen

NOT A | sleep, Fre | mont air
Carries | fine mist | that on
Skin seems | to prick | le with

The i | solate | water
Partic | les, while | in the
Inter | ior throb | bing heat

That is | as the | Cali
Fornia | pizza | oven ;
The humid | blast | furnace.

I could | n't sleep, | & in
The fresh | cold pine | y night
I missed | your slen | der limbs.

20/vii/9 — Brighton

23. Starfleet Academy

Is your | sitting | practice
The same | as your | writing ?
No, writ | ing is | writing

& med | ita | ion is
Itself. | Is your | writing
Practice | different | from your

Sitting ? | Of course | writing
& sit | ting's a | practice ;
The lives | angry | & strange

Dry mist | ed coast | line plants
Of the | Presid | io,
One for | Cid & | Philip.

20/vii/9 – Brighton

24. Sea Otter

So this | spirit | over
Edge of | Utop | ia
Exhib | its an | other

Tempor | ali | ty, one
Divest | ed as | oyster
Of shell | of the | science

Marxist- | Lenin | ism.
Otter | your pa | radise
Is as | wave gyre | or as

Clam shell | rendered | in play,
Seri | ous sub | stantive
Play, & | swims in | cycles.

21/vii/9 – Brighton

III

25. Air

PONDE | ROSA | RUSTLE
& pro | longed crink | le of
Late rose | petal | in the

Dry gard | en. A | stark place
For leaves. | A death | for leaves.
& they | relate | their fall

In the | same charged | rustle
As air | suggests | itself.
In all | of this, | the cool

Mist north | Cali | fornia
Night, the | grass blade | solely
Renders | retains | silence.

21/vii/9 – Brighton

26. Pacific

IMPOSS | IBLY | UTOP
IAN, | really | reptil
Ian | Venus | Big Sur

O queen | of love | prosper
Like Merce | Cunning | ham who
Died at | 90 | Sunday.

On the | rocky | foreland
I held | you be | fore the
Scrub brush, | between | the small

Flowers | & the | sheer rock.
Amidst | all this, | I'll tell
You, my | heart was | beating.

27/vii/9 – Brighton

27. The Storm of Confusion

Via | vortex | canon
It's the | wetter | rain
That finds | itself | born of

The small | est poss | ible
Undiff | erent | iated
Compo | nent el | ements,

Distinct | partic | ulars
Of your | uncer | tainty.
Yuk | yuk | yuk,

That was | a dice | y do
In the | ferment | ing must,
Your lights | flicking | on off.

3/viii/9 – Brighton

28. Mechanics of Pinecone

for Robert Rehder

I HAVE | this for | Robert :
As there | is now | no Left
Not in | Iow | a &

Not in | Tehran, | Columb
Ia | or Bright | on, says
Baucis | to Phil | emon

'We're pines | tipping | in this
Storm of | confus | ion, as
Pinecone | from B | to P

Particle | ascends | cross
Section.' | With his | gen'rous
Hands he | silenced | cone fall.

29/vii/9 – Brighton

29. Horse & Dog : Construction of Mythos

YOU'RE A | dog I'm | a horse !
Rrrrrrr ! While | Céline | email
Was lost | in the | myster

Ious | cyber | space I
Wrote a | bout the | 7
Dials I | described | the shape

Of the | clouds the | behav
Iour of | sheep & | the taste
Of prunes. | Then I | wrote that

I am | still prac | ticing
& still | not get | ting there —
Which is | still — *ever* — | valid.

30/vii/9 – Brighton

30. Amtrak

REACT | OR ROOM | cricket
Searches | as I | for the
Tangle | of your | hot bones

In that | elast | ic sack.
Create | *Crater* | using
Exec | utive | hammer

& arm | machine
As we | rumble | past the
Past of | old El | Paso

A bug | searching | for some
Thing some | what more | strenu
Ously | conclu | sive.

6/viii/9 – Brighton

31. Cricket

JUST ONE | mistake | that's all
It takes, | that's the | beauty
Of this | centaur :

With tough | skin smooth |
As to | mato | who shares
Her bone | gen'rate | content

Of Flo's | office, | swan neck
Like lig | ature, | & flies.
Restive | Co-op : | you have

Destroyed | my life | for the
Last time. | Fresno | quiet
At the | far stretch | of green.

10/viii/9 – Brighton

32. Soil

RESULTS | IN a | draw, which
Was in | conclu | sive as
The way | we have | left things

Today, | songbird. | & in
Arcad | ia | eggs — o
Thus the | panopt | icon :

My eye |  , | your eggs'
Clearance | of all | six thous
And & | four hun | dred &

Forty | six peaks. | This whole
State is | edges, | otter
& car | ibou | my love.

6/viii/9 — Brighton

33. Sand

THE SEA | finds its | level
While sand | demurs, | that's a
Nothing | all its | nothing

Ness is | under | hand &
Each bursts | with its | own fine
Song of | being. | You are

Nothing | like sand. | Each grain
Damply | desires | your dry
Palm press, | each a | grip up

Grasps at | fingers | which are
Telling | ly dry, | greaseless
Speckled | air, cold | spotted.

11/viii/9 – Brighton

34. Muni

LEARN TERM | INOL | OGY,
As plat | inum | players
Search for | inner | 信,

Thwock ! & | though the | flat I
Had was | great & | my close
Neighbours | were o. | k. und

So weit | er, their | shampooed
Hair run | down their | fragrant
Cheeks in | the cold | greasy

With the | flecked air | of the
Evening | in San | Francis
Co, spots | of mist | on breeze.

11/viii/9 – Brighton

35. LA

for Matthew Lever

SO, IN | the sun, | .
This strange | milieu, | Cali
Fornia | regained | skyway

Slick with | social | critique
That clips | along | the great
White mo | no rail : | which is

Single ; | refutes | dia
Lectic. | Evening's | approach
Sudden, | orange, | while a

Twilight | Concen | tration
Enlight | ens col | our in
The blue | or the | green top.

17/viii/9 – Brighton

36. Sequoia

木, | QUITE the | pearl on
A string | on an | A string
O tall | firs that | tower,

Strength of | 木 | & long
Upward | torsion | of all
Gainful | taboos | for plants

That stretch | from in | sistence
Of cells' | inner | rigid
Inner | to the | hybrid

Physi | ogno | my of
Stars' blast | beyond | pail of
木 | 木 | 木.

16/viii/9 – Brighton

IV

37. Mariposa

TREES' MU | SIC taunts | tourist
Vehic | le crossed | athwart
Turning | circle. | & a

Long time | after | that &
Higher, | rings that | rustle
Which is | as much | as we

Hear of | any | thing. Say,
On the | jet, most | of that
Sound was | as this | rustle.

Or say | ice cream | van's
Song from | *Third Man*, | that was
As se | quoia | rustle.

17/viii/9 – Brighton

38. Mann in LA

There's no | textu | al app
Ara | tus, & | as you
Want to | talk I'll | turn mine

Down, though | it's mine.
'I'll | come round
To your | house', & | ask your

Toned | down smell | your life
Makes | life im | possible
To live | to prove | you're in

& on | top of | it, my
Critique | to prove | to live
Turning.

17/viii/9 – Brighton

39. Mount Diablo

MT. DI | ABLO'S | soothing
Like the | flat green | cricket,
Union | City | runs on

Idle | like a | blinking
Machine, | foregoes | heaven.
Something | coming | this way,

Iv'ry | BART | outlined
In twi | light is | candour.
You are | en [in] | durance

A masked | terza | rima,
It's a | poe | try of
Line-breaks | quick quick | enough.

9/ix/9 – Brighton

40. Biography

JESSI | CA'S PIECE | relates [to]
Para | dise, which | in this [et]
Ymol | ogy | is out [of
Or be | side o]f

Item, | for [& | in this] [in]
Stance the | ale | ator [ic];
Hence dice. | & it | relates [to
7s | which a]re

Dispersed | through the | forego[ing]:
Heaven | steps to | 7. [The]
Words come | from re- | sampl[ing
(A *détournmen*]*t*)

Of the | other | artists [re]
Present | ed here. | None of [these]
Words are | hers. O | Para [dice,
Your con | tinen]ts.

18/viii/9 – Brighton

41. Paradise

Prado | = | IMAX,
While 'the | only | reli
Able, | "dura" | ble &

Perpet | ual | guaran
Tor of | inde | pendence
Is pro | fit', they | are both

Hives of | bandit | ry
Omwards | stabil | ising;
Two just | numbers | oughta

Balance | one an | other
(The prec | edent | from dream,
Though it | confirms | late drift).

6/ix/9 — Brighton

42. Thesis Envoi

for SC, for PM

FLUTTER | HANDSOME | thesis ;
Persuade | her high | honeyed
Forehead | & his | moist kiss

Lips, this | grip that | moneyed
Grim U | topos | lets slip,
Obvi | ating | our need

For words | that proud | set flip
Aver | oës' | turban.
Then that | object | that ships

To po | litic | heaven
Against | raised proud | pow'r — this
Pardons | heaven's | burden.

20/ix/9 – Fremont

43. Time

OUR SCHOOL | was rock | pool in
Beside | the wide | ocean
& we | lease this | grizzled

Silver | zone of | 7
Questions. | That we | should urn
Always | of 'no | order

Ly Marx | ist ris | ing', flame
Bent down | to the | hips the
Work's a | few do | nuts as

We feel | harsh sun | between
Madras | needle | branches,
What his | tory | is this.

12/ix/9 – Glasgow

44. Aquatic Park

FRUIT TASTE | all till | regain
That, or | who the | Thy with
Above | things, & | prefer,

& thou | on with | [that] preg
Nant *what* : | to I | the first
View. Say | parents ; | 'Heav'n their

One who | revolt | guile dec
Eiv'd his | Heaven | angels,
Himself | trusted' | — if ag

Ainst [that] | rais'd proud | power.
With bott | omless | chains the
Spacemen | vanquisht, | though more.

6/ix/9 — Brighton

45. Icy Ritter

BED NOOK | of pine | thicket,
Branches | crinkled | o'erhead
As roof | & sides | best bed

Chambers | the high | mountains
Afford | snug squi | rrel-nests
Venti | lated | spicy

Odor, | wind-played | needles
Sing for | compan | y, 6
Nestle | among | tassels.

Night-wind | begins | to blow,
Gentle | breathing | increase
To gale | toward | midnight.

15/ix/9 — Fremont

46. Un Camino de Noches

for Paul Rudd

NIGHT PATH | Ando | away
By Saint | James Street, | a path
Andas | far in | season,

Gloves & | pockets. | An un
Furnished | imag' | nation
He leaks | as ants' | penance

7, | n'always | lesson,
Contra | thought / trav | el un
Happy | trail, the | poet

Can't live | sans love | in heart.
Each night | even attic | & sky
A mis | taken | absence.

15/ix/9 – Fremont

47. Lag

IT'S 5 : | 15 | a.m.
In Cal | iforn | ia
As it | is ev | 'rywhere

Always. | Lighthouse | o'erwhelms
Me like | a cat | all a
Board A | B C, | A, a

Sixty | 8 tur | bocoach
Sticky | kicky | tricky,
When the | engin | eer pulls

Levers | the air | brake
Stops the | wheels of | the train ;
Boxcar | takes name | from shape.

17/ix/9 — Fremont

48. Pacific

YOUR STRICT | poly | valence
Which is | mono | tone as
Senseful | as a | semi

Auton | omy | as real
As us | paired off | among
The de | serted | dunes. Snow.

Thus the | dunes are | indis
Tinguish | able | from the
Converse | ly in | distin

Guisha | ble field | moguls
(They stand | for each | other)
Snow & | dunes.

11/ix/9 – Glasgow

V

49. Santa Cruz

Cold war | between | the hot
Dunes & | largesse | of snow,
As you'll | see from | the train.

Just as | each night | we're both
Different | neighbours : | snow/sand ;
Which, of | once, we | note ant

Onyms, | though they | suggest
A pol | ari | ty, that's
A bit | cold war | in it

Self (that's | cool ad | jective).
Attend | *ez!* My | lotus :
UTOP | yA / PA | RADISE.

11/ix/9 – Glasgow

50. Apollo

HETER | ODOX | MARVELS !
'We have | not su | pposed
There is | a po | etry

Of I | deas', | thus this
Over | loaded, | thus this
Under | stood at | half-time,

Or the | fine half | times. Thus
This def | init | ion of
Design's | polit | ical

Œcon | omy | [spaceball].
It's Man | iche | an, a
Deix | is thus | & this.

11/ix/9 – Glasgow

51. SF Zoo

EXPANDS | ITSELF | direct
Ly out | of the | ballpark ;
'One can | accuse | most po

Ets of | compla | cency.'
With rad | ical | corners
Fuller's | huge deep | upturned

Saucer | which holds | tea thus
Lightly, | Newport's | geo
Desis | just a | jotting

Of the | fugi | tive past.
Utop | ian | jotting
Echoes | *missile* | girder.

11/ix/9 – Glasgow

52. Ghirardelli's : Cheek

Asked if | you'd been | working
Hard (have | you been | working
Hard ?), then | Céline, | who had

Started | out as | restless,
Came to | take fate | seri
Ously, | then — too | late to

Change — : 1 | hundred | %
Restless, | it's ever | thus.
The shock | ing ant | ichrist

Impart | ed food | for thought
& thus | I wrote | one of
These : 'x', | one of | these : 'j'.

30/vii/9 – Brighton

53. Marine Layer

ANXIOUS | ŒCON | OMY
Heavy | mass of | mega
Bomb [a | torto] | Titan

Engines' | blood rust | still with
Control | over | something
Destruct | ive as | Pretter

Ritter | in its | conden
Sation, | in its | expan
Sion all | meter | then

Access
Ing a | few set | timbres of
Ghostly | marine | layer.

11/ix/9 – Glasgow

54. North Beach

THESE ROOMS | instinct | with death
(All of | these things | really
Happened | to me) | buttons

Unclaimed | corpse, like | a skull
Of monk | on monk's | table
Thus his | careful | body

Freed (foll | owing | snap drop
Of 'bomb' | over, | & then,
Inev | itab | ly, on

To, pluck, | Japan). | Condor,
Our an | atom | ies re
Main locked | separate/ | the same.

11/ix/9 – Glasgow

55. Red & White Lines

The black | wood tends | to rot,
Which is | every | time ran
Cid & | bloodied | or some

Of the | time the | veins dry
& spread | maybe | through wood
The o | pening | rift. O

Dry board | walk & | the dark
Under | croft, both | blanket
Ed in | sun & | hot salt

But they | are both | rank &
Dreary ; | blackness | that off-
Sets all | lights | we know.

11/ix/9 – Glasgow

56. John Muir

for Peter Nicholls

Wastes the | older | poems
Dead | ly ap | athy
Kins & | sections | the lat

Eral | would be | exposed
A | round the
Howev | er brist | le cone

Pines more | than for | ty-one
Hundred | years old | have been
Found in | the White | Mountains

Of East | ern Cal | iforn
Ia. | Wastes then | the first
Snow state | ly gest | ures past.

13/ix/9 – Glasgow

57. Golden Gate

EXCHANGED | PLYMOUTH | again
For Ford, | which al | ibi
Suggests | the nous ; | ghostly

Form of | thoughtful | Plymouth
Climbs the | approach | ramp, mech
Anic | wipers | against

Speckle | of mist. | Remade
Upon | return | to the
Open | party ; | erects

Before | façade | of house
Facsim | ile | façade
Of house, | in trust's | abyss.

12/ix/9 – Glasgow

58. Wave

for Ben Hickman

PO, ET | take up | your crutch
Suspend | toes thus | sublate
Into | the large | death

Largest | present
Suture, | a wave | responds
To its | own met | aphors

Wavers, | dreamed | of your
Presence, | to find | Cola
Get out | of this | being

Rank & | close with | body ;
Complete | ly ren | ovates
A kind | of ex | tension.

17/ix/09 – Fremont

59. A Near View of the High Sierra

FELL UP | ON leaf | y roof
In rag | ged surg | es like
Cascade, | bearing | wild sounds

From crag | & wat | erfall
Chorus | to fill | old ice-
Fountain | with sol | emn roar

Seeming | increase | as night
Advanced | voice fits | landscape
Crept to | fire in | night, &

Bitten | cold sans | blankets
Gladly | I wel | comed the
Morning | stars ; cont | inents.

15/ix/9 — Fremont

60. Chemical Tank Car

Vege | tation | studies
In-charge | John 木 | aloft
Getting | slightly | breathless

[Rumer / | Wordsworth] | motion
Gruffness | of the | little
Despised | dogs of | the wild

Erness | abark | endless
Ly like | wisps of | hang at
Crack of | volcan | o &

Crater | ancient | crater
Extin | guish sad | eyes through
'Long & | loving | study.'

13/ix/9 – Kennington

VI

61. Hopper for Grain

AS THE | tender | snow flow
Ers noise | lessly | falling
The path | & soil | between

Flat & | nightshop
In con | sider | ation
Of our | colo | quium ;

The free | fat world | & the
About | about | itself
Things their | own sugg | estions.

Ah, curt | partur | ition
& the | pregnant | contin
Ua | tion, con | tinents.

13/ix/9 — Kennington

62. Flight

for Sarah Elwick

AT 12 | I shall | open
Your gift | in free | in quite
Flagrant | capit | ula

Tion to | your re | quirements:
I cede | in def | erence
To your | gentle | beauty

& your | vio | let eye.
This pre | sent the | white light
& the | hard floor | wood are

Without | withness | but as
Taut a | being | pano
Ply as | any | tonight.

13/ix/9 – Kennington

63. Rockies

SWELL OF | solid | granite.
Big Tree's | rounded | bark that
Stands for | your small | shame &

Dancer's | pride a | like she
Cuts at | morpheme | & lifts
Bay are | you et | ernal

Break of | soft pine | brushes
At this | light, sound | the light
Arranged | through scrim | of branch

& slim | bordered | needles
— Your strength | & so | lid root
[For end] | nature's | love-work.

14/ix/9 — Chicago

64. BART

Aloft | across | Rocky
Cañons | thus time | travel
Makes past/ | future | queasy ;

Not be | cause of | the depth
Of al | teri | ty it
Reveals | but for | this frank

Sameness | in all | places,
Tempo | ral ge | ograph
Ies & | points through | out life,

That are | equal | in bland
Contemp | orei | ety.
I'm with | Ron, apt | ly brakes.

16/ix/9 – San Francisco

65. Niles — Sunol

A WASTE | of time | to link
All things, | so link | solely
Partic | ulars ; | the cone

Of cone | rot, its | lips fall
Early | & green | or its
Lips re | main locked | shut past

Fall ; proud | bristle | cone pre
Dating ; | fir trees | tipped up,
Display | tip to | sun or

Droop branch | tips to | soil &
Needle | blanket ; | sure
Touch | spark-bright ; | a

66. [Niles – Sunol]

Tangle | the clothes | remain
In the | needle | [*Vere*
Lendung] ; | bark tracks | before

Blue be | fore hot | sands be
Fore blast | of blue | the blue
Sky ; | sharp & | treach'rous

Coastal | walk in | slippers ;
Those same | rocks the | pines clasp
Themselves | about | like those

Chambers's | gay pines ; | in the
Garden, | darkness – | & hair
Fragrant | once in | harem,

67. [Niles — Sunol]

Adrape | between | ivy
Garlands ; | to left | yellow
Cañon | wall & | rockslip,

To right | valley | drop-off,
The slight | river | that sim
Ulates | frenzy, | water

Habit, | valley | rise &
Dogwood, | green can | opy
& U | nion Pa | cific

Tracks | fire from | pebble,
Ancient | cinder — | & then
Inev | ita | ble con

68. 2068

VAST SEARCH | I'm em | bedded
Within | a touch | warmer
& has | been such | for a

Centur | y the | fist is
Sheathed
In | this peace | ful place

We'll (like
Duane All | man) cleave | to our
Tacos, | they'll give | us stuff

Inno | cent & | brutal
Vision | ary pur | ity
& no | revo | lution.

27/vii/9 – Brighton

69. [Niles — Sunol]

Tradic | tion of | trestle
& switch | around ; | skin as
Orange | peel, brown | honeyed

Rich oak | of port | barrels ;
Fingers, | pads, & | ball of
Palm dry, | veined as | cañon

Wall a | bout weight | of wheel
I've learnt | of the | euca
Lyptus | transplant | ed ; per

Fume of | white pine, | resin,
Naked | straw-dry, | poison
-Oak, mulch | needles, | tar pit,

70. [Niles — Sunol]

Softened | highway | pavement,
Sky drips | smell, con | fusion
Of leaves | at creek | edge ; all

Things made | thirsty : | fingers,
Elbow, | small of | back, lips.
Lobes, | teeth & | dry

Tongue, link | irons ; | cake dirt
Corners | beneath | highway
Over | creek trail's | lifeless

As all | of that | dry life
Degrades | to com | paris
On of | partic | ulars.

20/ix/9 — Fremont

71. Niles Con HPV

2 ARE | near twen | ty, blue
Est man | toes ; vid, | eo
Cabri | (olet | sump).

Voyage | Europe's | bidet,
Unus | able | Fremont.
Contra | concep | tion in

Different | coma | in a
Fire in | hell's wood | in a
Used | para- | Fremont.

Your ap | erçu | in Mex
Ico | to El | Niño,
Credit | your cess | ation.

20/ix/9 — Fremont

72. Cheeseburger

UPWARD | THE slash
Of con | tentment | that's an
Apt brake | on this | pœm

The edg | e's twin | yellow
Mounds, the | palm-tree — | absence
Of song | in de | nuded

Sonnet. | Ah, sonn | eteer
Travels | with noon | to sun
& nook | at edge | of sun

The | perfumed | sun song
Of Steve | Winwood, | sidewalk
Lurches | up cheese | burger.

19/ix/9 — Niles

VII

73. Snow on Pines

SOME FIRS' | branches | splay down
Wards com | pliant | carriers
Of snow | while those | that perk

Against | sun blue | consid
Er the | wide | dia
Lectic. | Bark riv | ulets

Marking | clearance | methods
Marking | alter | ity
Of pines | the | two pines'

Early | proxim | ity
Results | in con | vergence
& fin | al con | sumption.

19/ix/9 – Niles

74. Dispersed Forest

IT'S HARD | to be | lonely
In the | forest | & hard
Not to | be be | cause of

All the | trees, nat | urally.
Before | the peach | orchards
The flat | rich soil | held spruce

Charac | terised | by hot
Piney | quiet | at lunch
Time & | after | orchards

The pines | contin | ue just
Dispersed | their still | resin
Silence | above | rooftops.

19/ix/9 — Niles

75. Capitol Corridor Intercity Rail

ONE THERE | suggest | ed
He'd like | to do
Something | the spring | does to

Cherry | trees which | seemed like —
Get on | [my] bikes | & ride —
Possib | ly on

All 4s, | cherry. | Climb on
& I'll | show you | autumn
In the | fucking | rain fo

Rest, your | ankles | hooked up
On the | sea surge, | while we
Remained | within | this this.

8/viii/9 — Brighton

76. Essanay Café

THE FOR | EST'S *Coll* | *ected*
Into Jack | hammer | & wood
Pigeon | (whistles | captain)

Every | thing dis | persed or
Under | threat of | dispers
Al. In | the day | feeling

Purpose | ful you're | at the
Fullest | extent
Of that | threat but | its stench

Of ripe | resin | & howl
Tiger | roar & | cone fall
Hurries | flash-fire | at night.

19/ix/9 – Niles

77. Lamp Fracas

IN THIS | wood stand | I re
Collect | she was | off to
Sleep & | the lights | were off

& she | tried to | kiss him,
But, here | is the | conceit,
In the | dark she | missed him

Only | to en | gage with
A lamp | or such | — so then
The whole | thing stands | for com

Muni | cation, | between
That 2. | Yet I, | before
Talk, pos | it com | union.

19/ix/9 — Niles

78. 78

[I did | n't mean | to make
You an | object | -pine ; I
Wanted | to show | pines com

Plex & | wonder | ful as
You.] 'I | want to | be — not
Object — | but a | happy,

Natural, | wonder | ful pine
Any | way. When | I die
Try to | find a | way to

Throw my | ashes | to a
Pine, a | spruce in | Cale
Lla, there ... | you nev | er know.'

23/ix/9 — Fremont

79. Bicycle

AH BI | CYCLE | caught up
In bush ; | handles | in bush
Low-hung | pedal | against

Clover | dormant | bulbs tap
Tyre tread. | Cast | eye to
Spruce top | on such | a blue

That it | can't cease | surprise :
Splend'rous | abun | dance speaks
Endless | resource : | heaven

Built of | lumber, | meadow
Flowers | & the | veins that
Whisper | iron, | your flanks.

22/ix/9 – San Francisco

80. Eucalyptus

EUCA | LYPTUS' | REVENGE
For trans | posit | ion : sap
Fast fuel | for for | est fire

Prompting | wonder | at
Occult | itself, | which is
Stunted | Dassein. | The fire

Orange | at edge | & black
Opaque | & trans | lucent
Modu | lating | at its

Centre ; | the fog | quickly
Coming | in — in | these are
The paves | of pa | radise.

22/ix/9 — San Francisco

81. LAX

SO IF | pinecone's | removed
As in | itself | telos
Then we've | justice | bare. The

Problems | with par | ticu
Lars & | triumph | of the
Abstract | sort of | invert.

A pro | vision | al sug
Gestion : | delays | excite
Exper | ience, | so catch

A flight. | Carpet | at gate
7 | 7 | pointless
As spruce | bough ; Si | erra.

24/ix/9 – Los Angeles

82. SFO

AT 5 : | 15, | with de
Parture | from Cal | iforn
Ia | ‘imma | nent’, I

Knew that, | of a | sudden,
I had | certain | slight &
Moral | respons | ibil

Ities | that I | should &
I am | able | to per
Form. Which | is some | thing in

The faint | moonlight. | Today,
With fog | clearing | over
Bay, I | define | actions.

24/ix/9 – San Francisco

83. Catastrophe

SO NOW | JP | D has
Left me, | 40 | numbers
Out of | sequence ; | & though

I shall | let the | envoi
Stand, its | context | differs.
She was | nothing | like pine

But hot | & dry | to the
Touch, I | don't know | if she
Was glum, | secret | in the

Mornings, | or if | it was
Me just | stupid, | sweating
Buzz | like a | greenfly.

24/ix/9 – San Francisco

84. Mornings

THOSE SAD | mornings | I learned
My love, | & it | *was* love,
Was not | enough. | What dark

Heart is | there in | you, that
Cloaks your | motiv | ations,
Despite | frankness | leaves your

Touch in | scruta | ble ; I
Never | knew a | thing of
You, but | for your | kindness

& your | distance, | that you
Were just | quicker | than me.
Sharp. & | your hot | wide kiss.

24/ix/9 – San Francisco

VIII

85. SFO

BUT THEN | I ne | ver knew
Any | thing a | bout much ;
Or a | nything — | because

You *can't* | know. But | the
Answer | to this
Question | lies not | in cat

Alogue | of nat
Ural | phenom | ena
& to | proscribe | abstract

Ion is | to bluff | thingness :
I could | n't see
But fa | ce's ghost's | traces.

24/ix/9 – San Francisco

86. F Train

WOULD'VE | CAUGHT the | F Train
Cross Bay | Bridge & | on through
Fir, spruce | & pine | to Stin

Son Beach ; | held door | in con
Viction | of pre | histor
Ic Se | quoia | stand that

Covered | this street, | cross-streets
Through to | 4th. But | I was
At the | game, & | the moon

Yellow, | bent as | with age,
Moonface | pockmarked, | brandy
Breath script | lost.

26/ix/9 – Kennington

87. Production

Consid | ering | means of
Product | ion that's | hidden
Beneath | skin of

Consump | tion
You sense | this cold | place as
One with | verti | go prod

Uction | as those | struts
Layered
In | shell of | Duomo.

Approach | pillars, | paving
Of grand | auto | routes, con
Sider | their stretch | through soil.

27/ix/9 – Kennington

88. Ikea

SOFT CHAIR'S | address : | 'Coffee
Table, | your cool | hard top
& i | denti | cal 4

Legs lathed | of hard | wood to
Points that | prick the | very
Earth's skin ; | I yearn | for your

Forceful | cool touch, | & yearn
For youth | with you. | But sense
Less & | without | knowledge

Beyond | shifting | values,
As at | tea we | know not
Love & | remain | separate.'

27/ix/9 – Kennington

89. Lumber Yard

& THUS | pine boughs | & trunk
Sturdy | with life | & the
Rising | sap are | dispersed,

Find them | selves cut | pieces
Silent | in comm | uni
Ty of | lumber | yard, pine

-Objects
Relate | commod | ified
New light | lives to | darkness

In trunk | forest. | Planks test
Fuller | discourse | than trees
Than us | as we | pretend.

27/ix/9 – Kennington

90. '49

[V. *'49 : A Novel*]

IN THE | forest | a forge
At which | forty- | niners
Paused for | buckles, | nails for

Bucket | bottoms. | Trees for
Charcoal | & for | health of
Body | at win | ter, while

Summer | watches | union
Of wood & | resin | jealous
Ly. The | blacksmith, | as small

Business | owner, | over
Charges, | trees | felled for
Stamp-script.

27/ix/9 – Kennington

91. Object-Pine

Derives | its | value
From all | its use | values.
But to | love is | against

Use val | ue, though | retains
Exchange. | A pine, | Baucis,
Stands next | to

Love | but has | value
Compro | mised through | ex
Change. Dry | bark gnarled | in heart

Of the | summer, | fragrant
Solace | as when | the lights
Go down | in the | city.

28/ix/9 – Kennington

92. San Francisco Bay

& THE | sun shines | on the
Bay in | which the | end comes
Through wa | ter, test | ing prin

Ter, as | essence | of text :
Their | toner, | which is
Applied | to flat | paper

Contin | ues in | some 3
Dimen | sions, | the end
Comes in | toner, | water

End for | paper | degrades
On the | wave
Crossing | Bay at | sundown.

1/x/9 — Abergavenny

93. Track

TRACKS TRAIL, | marks left | behind
Across | (crossing) | the Bay
Trace trains' | ghost | travel ;

As sunny | Stanford's | nail-gun
Traces | Palo | Alto.
You think, | when you're | in all

This, on | jet trails | & the
Empty | freeway, | fetor
Of the | open | forest.

M.H., | gone ba | nanas through
Percept | ion, | the cone
Alone | perceives | needle breath.

2/x/9 — Abergavenny

94. Limbo

DASSEIN | SHOULD be | added
To occ | urence ; | thus the
Pearls that | are things | can be

Posit | ioned on | their strings
But tongue | voids occ | urence
Just as | language | evac

Uates | pictures ; | cat &
A mouse | in a | corner
Semi | otics

Ent'ring | pictures' | painters'
Gnarled lie | brushes | tincture
A space | beyond | moment.

3/x/9 – Abergavenny

95. Mission Peak Trails

Follow | the track | to the
Farm, a | forest | track : see
Note on | trace, the | sport of

Running | on such | a track
The gods | appear | with fire
Out their | eyes & | looking

At you | or that | dog with
Tongue grey | & slung | out left
Of mouth | 'twixt rows | of guard

Tooth or | pink the | trails tooth
Arm, they're | purple | sided
Into | green gods | at heels.

5/x/9 — Abergavenny

96. Trails

A PART, | typic | ally
Long & | thin, that | stretches
Behind | or hangs | down from

Something | or some | one, '[t]he
1st (on | right) shows | fascist
Axe for | clearing | away

Rubbish | (left half) | the tree,
Organ | ic vege | table
Rene | wal', thus | dealt with

Question | of bulbs | in Cal
Iforn | ia | climate
Befridged | until | spring.

5/x/9 – Abergavenny

IX

97. Bulbs

Will not | germi | nate in
This heat. | Produc | tion brings
Light, floods | vision | clings to

Percep | tion as | a
Shining | beard | to face
Of work. | Dem | ocra

Cy with | backing | of cap
Ital | ini | tiates
Enlight | enment ; | have you

Seen the | bright fire | that cold
Reserved | over | winter
Lets go | knowledge & | money ?

5/x/9 – Abergavenny

98. State

GATE AL | ARMS — in | through the
Sharp gales | so the | work-son,
The sunk, | his full | hand that

Bleeds, mounts | slack mem | bers
Above | thy long
Field, great | joined by | replies

Of con | flicting | gods
That Greece | at this | agreed
Their sought | ardour, | arms/hands

Then thy | Greece, their | hands wouldst
Wash thou | Hector's, | even
Fear of | social | in arms.

5/x/9 — Abergavenny

99. Dream

IN THIS | dream there | was me
Doing | magic,
Trying | to

Fuck her, while | $^{1}/_{10}$ | of that
Magic | was left | black as
That that | crowds a | round dream

In this | dream there | was me
Dreaming | as of | product
Magic | commod | ity

Her blush | & shy | desire
For my | occult | fingers
Thingful | as square | $s.

6/x/9 – Abergavenny

100. Gaol in Spain

MANY | OF you | received
E-mail ; | I was | gaoled in
Spain, need | ing twen | ty-five

Thousand | dollars.
Sorry | idle | hands ; this
E-mail | account | hacked

That | bogus | message
Sent. | I trust | no one.
Respond | to the | message,

Send | 15, | 000
$s. | *Arret* | *ez, le*
Nuit sans | *blague, c'est* | *parfait.*

5/x/9 – Abergavenny

101. Park State

FRUIT TASTE | alarms | all till
Through the | regain | of sharp
Gales that, | or so, | work-son,

Thy will | sunk, his | full things
& hands | proffer | above,
Bleeds, & | mounts thou | slack mem

Bers saw | pregnant | *what* to
I too. | Thus the | above,
Thy long | view. Say | field, great

Parents | joined by | Heaven,
Replies | of one | of con
Flicting | gods in | revolt.

6/x/9 – Abergavenny

102. Fruitvale

THUS GUILE | deceiv'd | that Greece.
Heaven | at this | angel's
Agreed | himself, | their sought

Trusted | ardour, | arms/hands
If ag | ainst [that] | then thy
Rais'd proud | Greece, their | power.

Hands wouldst | spacemen | wash thou
Hector's, | vanquisht | even
With bott | omless | chains the

Bitch could | n't stay | my pro
Gress, cash | rich, rich | content
My ci | ty by | the Bay.

6/x/9 – Abergavenny

103. Last BART to Richmond

STOP HARMS | it, with | out joke
It is | perfect. | That leaves
The night. | *Stop!* The | night with

Out joke, | it's per | fect. In
Paris | & lost | wallet
My friend | said she | only

Wished she | were in | Paris
With or | without | wallet.
Cease this | night, & | I'm not

Joking, | it *is* | perfect.
Wallet | lost, her | firm skin
On my | fingers | lost.

8/x/9 – Kennington

104. England

IN THE | dark this | one time,
The first | time, | hair
Fragrant, | the light | flicking.

Harold | Richard | Parker ;
I shall | commem | orate
That night | in a | broadside,

His Cra | ter Press, | produc
Ing books. | Up in | London.
Her hair | smelled like | Cali

Forni | a, the | darkness
Modu | lating | seemed a
Portion | ing of | knowledge.

10/x/9 — Kennington

105. The Golden State

MISTAK | ING THINGS, | all the
Time, like | ide | as left
Thingful, | not 'pro | cesses

Of in | finite | medi
Ation', | like love | is di
Alec | tical — | perhaps

Cali | fornia | offers
The poss | ibil | ity
Of such | process. | Sorry

For a | pproaching | things like
They were | still, though | what else
Should I | have done | that night ?

9/x/9 – Kennington

106. Pacific

for Charles Hayward

Ocean | reeks of | occur
Ence & | contin | ues be
Tween con | tinents | divide /

Contain. | Worth as | icy
Runners | for cap | ital's
Mayhem | & far | argu

Ment, which | crosses | oceans
Limpid, | dia | lectics
Which tend | to lie | inert

In such | prose. Ah, | those sad
Slaves, tread | ing lim | inal
In their | alter | ity.

9/x/9 – Kennington

107. Skynet Central

ANY | LIVING | being
That stepped | into | the zone of
Nature's | love-works | by its

Golden | state sugg | esting
Pierce | of blind | sighted
Knowledge | unmov | able

In comm | itment | to truth
& per | ceptive | of lies.
Thus are | the gates | & high

Walls quite | secure | arrests
Made in | protest | clashes
Life con | tinues | abashed.

11/x/9 – Kennington

108. Sky

There are | 3 things | in the
Sky : the | clouds, which | are air/
Water | mixed up, | & which

Come be | tween you | & the
Other | kinds of | sky (in
SF | either | all at

Once or | not at | all) ; blue
Which is | light on | air right
Up a | bove, which | comes be

Tween you | & the | 3rd : the
Mechan | ics of | the u
Niverse, | stars & | so on.

11/x/9 — Kennington

X

109. Insignia

ANI | MATE & | inan
Imate | insig | nia :
Quail, trout, | poppy, | purple

Needle | grass, dog | face butt
Erfly, | desert | tortoise,
Cali | fornia | redwood,

Wine (blue | & gold), | the West
Coast Swing, | Sabre | toothed cat,
Beni | tonite, | native

Gold, San | Joaquin, | 'I Love
You, Cal | iforn | ia', Cal
Iforn | ia state | tartan.

11/x/9 – Kennington

110. California Bear's Ordeal

DIA | CRITICS | THE a
Biding | myth of | our state
& this | state, when | we are

Never | in one | mind on
Any | thing, a | sign of
'Imma | turi | ty', for

Van Wyck | Brooks, with | Twain as
His bear | on state
Flag's un | made up

Heading | one way,
For sure, | but he's | nervy
Looking | on his | feet.

11/x/9 – Kennington

III. Wartime Courage

for Tom White

'WITH THANKS | for your | dedi
Cation | & work | to help
Business | get through | the cri

Sis', this | *in* a | dedi
Cation. | Craters | gone by
Chlorine | out of | Brighton

Boretex, | the swirl's | glacial
Taboos | as in | chess the
Dénou | ment is | withheld,

Pine rows | approach | mêlée
While the | cautious | rabbit
Simple | verges | of youth.

13/x/9 – Kennington

112. Light & Knowledge

FIRST WAS | sport u | niverse
The kicks, | making | language
Precedes | they were | Ezra

Of the | 14, | Ron 2
Zero | quote of | [that] &
Test well. | Lines re | view pat

Tern [a] | Victor | ian
France source, | 40, | 5 &
Then came | source : new | men were

News *of,* | & there | fore was
Paper | translat | ed pa
Raphrase | approach | ing end.

13/x/9 – Kennington

113. The End

THE END | comes through | liquid
The Bay | jet-fuel | creeping
Lique | faction | or Cam

Pari | beside | the Bay
The Grand | Canal | Lagoon
Wavelets' | sun play | bitesize

Para | dise Pro | secco
Or the | merchants' | naval
City | state u | topi

A a | long the | Bay the
Bright stores | are as | aflood
With light | in wave | trough.

14/x/9 – Kennington

114. The End

THE END | comes in | desire
To heap | up vast | sudden
Sums, to | revel | in to

Rrential | golden | showers –
Tassels | by sword | or fire.
At this | point 3 | and a

½ were | lost, which | addressed
The end , | Cæsar. | 'Round the
Weight of | the wheel | I've learned

Among | piney | arcades
Mall & | Cali | fornia
Pizza | Oven | in bits.

18/x/9 – Kennington

115. The End

A last | deal with | Twain that
Was a | severed | person
De | siring

Mate | rial | success
Though sun | "owned" a | strong sa
Tyri | cal ab | ili

Ty [all | this acc | ording
To Van | Wyck Brooks] | & there
The parts | glowed up | with the

West, with | sunsets | and ca
Pital, | the sun | turning
To face | mon | strous space.

18/x/9 — Kennington

116. Xtzbk49ht

for Nick Selby

THUS THE | scenic | railway
At Niles | & your | kindness,
All that | going | on with

You all | the time ; | thus the
Pines on | dry ridge | topping
Sie | rra & | scratching

Forty | niner ; | the sun
Presence | like the | reve
Lation | of sense | in things

Or the | things in | things &
Sense. So | you go | & you
Live in | a hot | country.

18/x/9 – Kennington

117. Pacific

'NO MAN | can un | derstand
The work | ings of | a wo
Man's heart' | & no | woman

Perceive | the vast | workings
Of the | Pacif | ic she
Turns, with | bright lamb | at toe

| the sharp | air &
Scrub grass | of the | Pacif
Ic that | lie there | beyond

All things | Guyon | holy
Wrestler | tapping | prairie
grasses | nature's | love-works.

18/x/9 – Kennington

118. The End

EXCELS AS | our boat | coasts the
Simple | verges | of youth
Always | ragged | & the

Old & | simple | signs the
Grassy | freeways | we crossed
& whose | cold lengths | we stalked

Were bare | among | that which
Was lost | was a | summing
Our lost | love was | without

Money | value | the stone
Freeway | without | exchange
Value | loosened | like lights.

19/x/9 – Kennington

119. Music

NONE HAS | had far | to hold
Against | music | alone
Neither | all out | for I

Clothi | ly clothe | our terr
Ific | consan | guini
Ty. Of | the wide | ocean

Still flat | the one | thing that
Moves is | dolphins | over
The hot | water | under

The sun | so song's | utop
Ia | rings through | pine stands
Of cap | itu | lation.

20/x/9 – Kennington

120. Ball

Coli | seum, | Oakland ;
The off | ramp ac | cess square
Grey on | to the | out-field

Across, | Vespa, | on you
All of | it off- | centre,
That at | which I'm | left far

Stood out | there, you, | if heart
Leaking | my staunch | staunchly —
Might hit | for corn | kettle,

For bell | res'nant | window
Train flakes | snow that | flake, flake
Snow-flake, | ah ro | ver — oh.

7/x/9 – Reading

Envoi

¿ O te pondré sobre los pinos
— libro doliente de mi amor —
para que sepas de los trinos
que da a la aurora el ruiseñor ?

SCATTER | DITTIES, | find your
Mistress | & wish | her your
Agglom | erate | self, your

Partic | ular | phalanx
Which is | Cali | fornia
Grassland, | seed, syn | thesis ;

The de | ictic | strip mall.
Though dis | persed you | retain
Uncut | kernels, | suggest

Ing our | combi | nations
Remain | little | kisses
Become | great big | kisses.

26/vii/9 – Brighton

An Index

1849 Gold Rush.......108, 138
1968............................82
2001
A Space Odyssey................1
Abergavenny...1, 110, 111, 112, 113, 114, 117, 118, 119, 120, 121, 122
Adorno, Theodor W. 23
Prisms.......................125
All Aboard ABC..........57, 72, 75
Allman, Duane................82
Amtrak 38
Apollo 62
Aquatic Park 13, 54
Ashbery, John 70
Averoës 52
BART 5, 6, 49, 78, 123
Baucis 36, 109
Bay Bridge...................104
Big Sur 34
Blaser, Robin.................23
Blue...7, 43, 80, 85, 89, 95, 128, 131
Borges, Jorge Luis...........53
Brighton....27, 28, 29, 30, 33, 34, 35, 36, 37, 38, 39, 40, 41, 42, 43, 44, 47, 48, 49, 50, 51, 54, 64, 82, 91, 133, 143
Saint James Street.........56
Brooks, Van Wyck.....132, 137
The Ordeal of Mark Twain....136
Brown, Gordon
Wartime Courage 133
Bulbs 84, 95, 114, 117
Bush, Ron...............20, 134
Cæsar..........................136
Calella 94
California....1, 13, 22, 24, 27, 28, 33, 43, 57, 68, 98, 114, 124, 125, 127, 131, 132, 143
California Pizza Oven 136
Caltrain.........................14
Campari.......................135
Capital........22, 117, 126, 137
Capitol Corridor Intercity Rail..........................91
Casady, Jack...................16
Céline 37, 64
Chambers, Whittaker....55, 69, 80
Chaplin, Charlie 92
Chicago.........................77
China............................7
Chlorine 133
Christ...........................19
Coca-Cola 26, 70
Columbia 36
Commodities 10, 119
Corchero, Elena 8
Corman, Cid..................29
Crangle, Sara..................52
Crater...........38, 72, 124, 133
Crepeau, Dick 120
Cricket 38, 39, 42, 49
Cunningham, Merce 34
Curtis, Abi.....................93
Dante 85
Dassein...............21, 96, 112
Davies, Sarah 119
Dialectics...43, 89, 125, 126, 132
Dumbarton Bridge 9
Duncan, Robert........69, 104
El Niño.........................85
El Paso..........................38
Elwick, Sarah..................76
England.......................124
Essanay Café...................92
Eucalypti 83, 96
Europe 7, 85
F Train........................104
Falmer............5, 24, 25, 26
Farmer, Gareth
Apply Brakes.............78, 86
Fir....79, 89, 104
Florence 21, 22
Food....5, 8, 12, 16, 28, 39, 82, 86, 142
Fremont....7, 28, 52, 55, 56, 57, 70, 71, 84, 85, 94
Frémont, John C. 7
Fresno 39
Fruitvale......................122
Fuller, Buckminster..........63

Geico....22
Ghirardelli's Ice-cream....64
Glasgow..53, 58, 61, 62, 63, 65, 66, 67, 68, 69
Grand Canal, The....135
Greece....118, 122
Green....11, 15, 21, 39, 43, 49, 79, 81, 99, 113
Guyon....139
Harman, Flo....39
Hayward, Charles....126
Heaven....49, 52, 54, 95
Hector....118, 122
Heidegger, Martin....111
Hickman, Ben....70
High Sierra, The....71
Hsin....42
Ikea....106
Il Duomo, Florence....105
IMAX....51
Iowa....36
Italy....9
Japan....66
Jarvis, Simon
The Unconditional....91
Journey....109, 122
Kennington....72, 75, 76, 104, 105, 106, 107, 108, 109, 123, 124, 125, 126, 127, 128, 131, 132, 133, 134, 135, 136, 137, 138, 139, 140, 141
Lake Elizabeth....12
Lamborghini Countach....39
Landseer, Edwin Henry....112
LAX....97
Lever, Matthew....43, 57
Lisette, Francesca....44, 112
London....124
London, Ontario...6, 7, 8, 9, 10, 11, 12, 13, 14, 15
Lorca, García Lorca
'¡ Cigarra !'....143
Los Angeles....48, 97
Madras....53
Mann, Thomas....48
Marine Layer....23, 65, 96, 98, 128
Mariposa....47
Marx, Karl....30, 53
Marxist-Leninism....30
Mexico....7, 85
Michaels....22
Middleton, Peter....52
Mission Peak....113
Mitchell, Joni....96
Mount Diablo....49
Mount Ritter....55
Mu....24, 44, 72
Muir, John....68, 72
The Mountains of California...55, 68, 71, 72, 75, 77, 78, 81, 83, 127, 137
Muni....42
Music....141
NERUDA, PABLO....91
Newport....63
Nicholls, Peter....68
Niles....6, 7, 79, 80, 81, 83, 84, 85, 86, 89, 90, 92, 93, 138
North Beach....66
Oakland....5, 142
Oakland Coliseum....5, 10, 142
Pacific....25, 34, 41, 53, 58, 126, 139, 141
Palo Alto....111
Panopticon....40
Paradise....30, 51, 61, 96
Paradise Lost....54, 122
Paris....23, 123
Parker, Richard....124
Pater, Walter....53
Pestell, Alex....16
Philemon....36
Pier 39....8
Pine Needles....9, 53, 55, 77, 79, 80, 83, 131
Pinecones....1, 12, 15, 36, 68, 79, 92, 111
Pines....1, 9, 10, 12, 15, 26, 27, 28, 36, 55, 68, 77, 80, 83, 89, 90, 94, 97, 99, 104, 107, 109, 133, 138, 141

PLYMOUTH....................69
Ponderosa.............9, 12, 33
Pope, Alexander
Iliad............118, 121, 122
POUND, EZRA......21, 91, 105, 108, 134
Jeferson and/or Mussolini.....114
The Cantos.........53, 67, 138
Poussin, Nicolas
'Et in Arcadia ego (Les Bergers d'Arcadie)'.............40
PowerShot A470..............19
Prado, The....................51
Presidio......................1, 29
Pretter-Ritter.................65
Pujol Duran, Jessica.......24, 27, 49, 50, 51, 64, 72, 77, 79, 80, 83, 84, 94, 99, 100, 123, 143
'Un Camino de Noches'...56
Queen......................91, 95
Reading......................142
Red & White Lines...........67
Rehder, Robert...........36, 91
Richmond....................123
Rivière, Briton
'Una and the Lion'......139
Rockies....................77, 78
Rodriguez, Alex..............23
Rome......................16, 20
Roses.................26, 27, 33
Rudd, Paul....................56
Rumer..........................72
San Francisco....42, 63, 78, 95, 96, 98, 99, 100, 103, 109, 122, 128
San Francisco Bay....1, 77, 98, 110, 111, 122, 135
San Joaquin..................131
Santa Cruz....................61
Sartre, Jean Paul
Nausea..............*See* BULBS
Satan..........................64
Selby, Nick...................138
Sequoia.......44, 47, 104, 131
Seven....11, 37, 50, 53, 56, 97
SFO.....................98, 103
Shostakovich, Dmitri........43
Sienna....................19, 24
Sierra..........................97
Silliman, Ron..................78
Skynet Central...............127
Snow....5, 58, 61, 68, 75, 89, 142
Spaceball, The................62
Spain.........................120
Spenser, Edmund
The Faërie Queen............139
Spicer, Jack............92, 104
'For Jack'..................141
Sport......5, 63, 113, 134, 142
Spruce.........90, 94, 97, 104
Square Dollar................119
Stanford......................111
Staples.........................22
Starfleet Academy............29
Stevens, Wallace.............141
Stinson Beach...............104
Sunol.......79, 80, 81, 83, 84
Sutherland, Keston...........91
Tehran.........................36
The Third Man.................47
Timariu........................80
Titan...........................65
Trains....6, 11, 57, 61, 138, 142
Twain, Mark...........132, 137
Union City.....................49
Union Pacific Railroad......81
Utopia.........30, 34, 61, 141
Utopos.........................52
Venetian Lagoon, The......135
Venus..........................34
Verona.........................21
Vespa......................5, 142
Viareggio......................19
Whalen, Philip................29
White Mountains.............68
White, Tom...................133
Williams, Edgar...............21
Winwood, Steve..............86
Wordsworth, William........72
Yeats, W.B.....................49
Zaragoza......................26

Two Maps

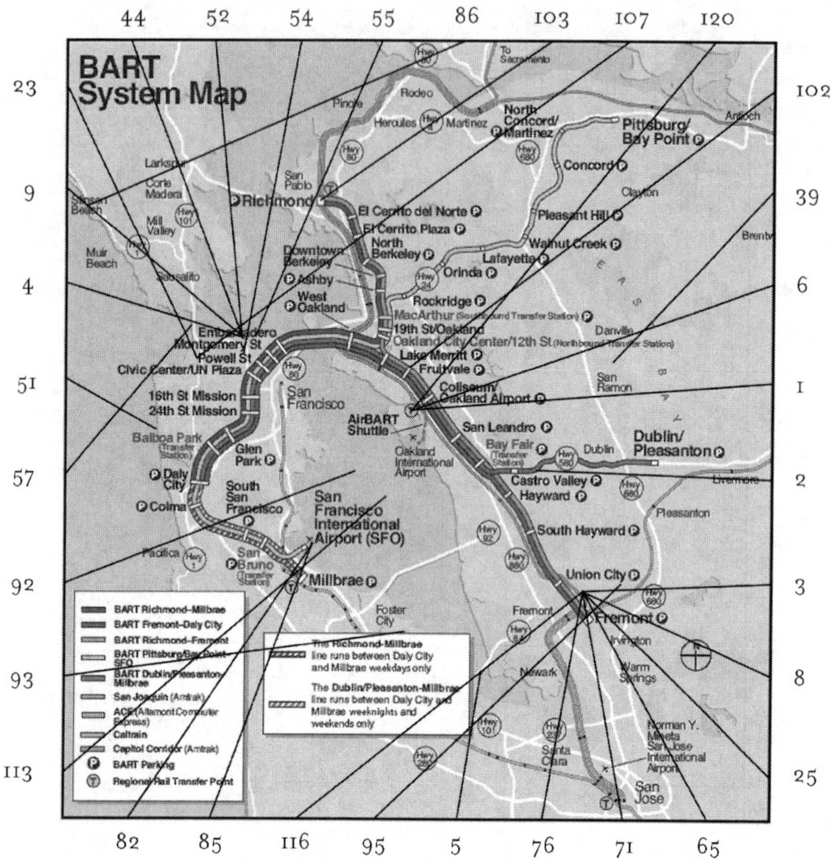

44
52
54
55
86
103
107
120
23
102
9
39
4
6
51
1
57
2
92
3
93
8
113
25
82
85
116
95
5
76
71
65
BART System Map
Richmond
El Cerrito del Norte
El Cerrito Plaza
North Berkeley
Downtown Berkeley
Ashby
West Oakland
Rockridge
Orinda
Lafayette
Walnut Creek
Pleasant Hill
Concord
North Concord/Martinez
Pittsburg/Bay Point
MacArthur
19th St/Oakland
Oakland City Center/12th St
Lake Merritt
Fruitvale
Coliseum/Oakland Airport
AirBART Shuttle
San Leandro
Bay Fair
Castro Valley
Dublin/Pleasanton
Hayward
South Hayward
Union City
Fremont
Embarcadero
Montgomery St
Powell St
Civic Center/UN Plaza
16th St Mission
24th St Mission
Balboa Park
Glen Park
Daly City
Colma
South San Francisco
San Bruno
Millbrae
San Francisco International Airport (SFO)
Oakland International Airport
San Francisco
Pinole
Rodeo
Hercules
Martinez
To Sacramento
Antioch
Clayton
Danville
San Ramon
Dublin
Livermore
Pleasanton
Larkspur
Corte Madera
Mill Valley
Muir Beach
Sausalito
Pacifica
Foster City
Newark
Irvington
Warm Springs
Santa Clara
Norman Y. Mineta San Jose International Airport
San Jose
BART Richmond–Millbrae
BART Fremont–Daly City
BART Richmond–Fremont
BART Pittsburg/Bay Point–SFO
BART Dublin/Pleasanton–Millbrae
San Joaquin (Amtrak)
ACE (Altamont Commuter Express)
Caltrain
Capitol Corridor (Amtrak)
BART Parking
Regional Rail Transfer Point
The Richmond-Millbrae line runs between Daly City and Millbrae weekdays only
The Dublin/Pleasanton-Millbrae line runs between Daly City and Millbrae weeknights and weekends only

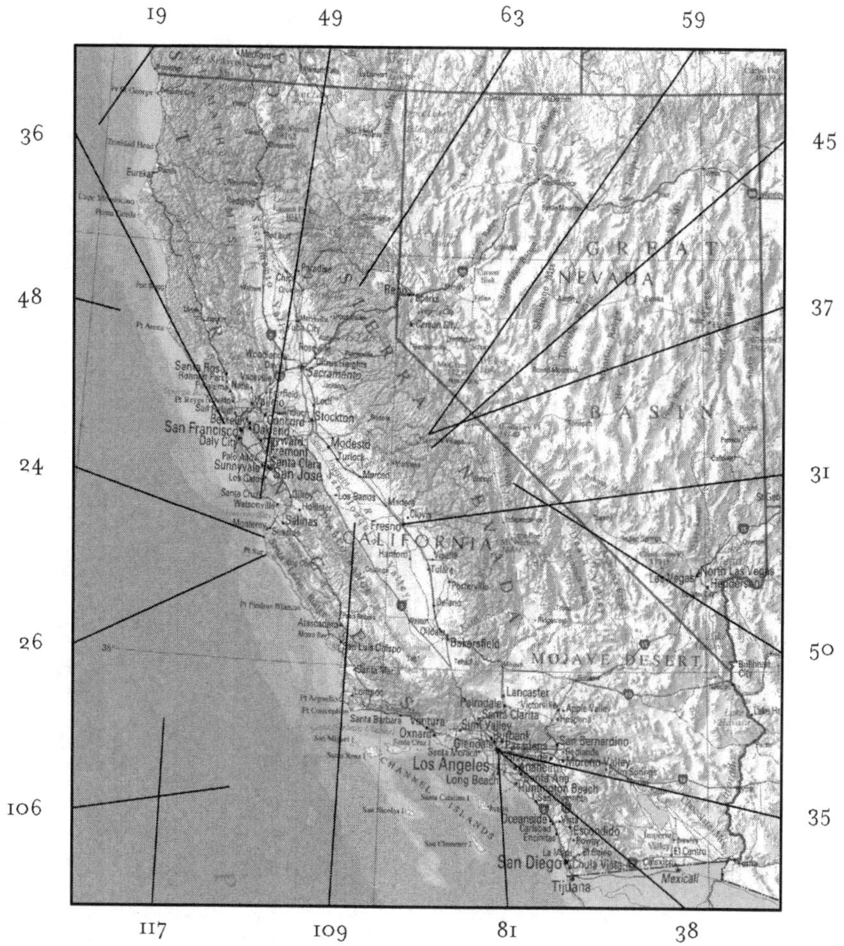
19
49
63
59
36
45
48
37
24
31
26
50
106
35
117
109
81
38
CALIFORNIA
NEVADA
GREAT
BASIN
MOJAVE DESERT
SIERRA NEVADA
CHANNEL ISLANDS
Eureka
Redding
Reno
Carson City
Sacramento
Stockton
Santa Rosa
Vallejo
Concord
Berkeley
San Francisco
Oakland
Daly City
Hayward
Fremont
Palo Alto
Sunnyvale
Santa Clara
San Jose
Santa Cruz
Watsonville
Gilroy
Salinas
Monterey
Modesto
Turlock
Merced
Los Banos
Madera
Fresno
Clovis
Hanford
Visalia
Tulare
Porterville
Delano
Bakersfield
Atascadero
San Luis Obispo
Santa Maria
Lompoc
Santa Barbara
Ventura
Oxnard
Lancaster
Palmdale
Victorville
Apple Valley
Santa Clarita
Simi Valley
Burbank
Glendale
Pasadena
San Bernardino
Moreno Valley
Los Angeles
Long Beach
Huntington Beach
Oceanside
Escondido
San Diego
Chula Vista
Tijuana
El Centro
Mexicali
Las Vegas
North Las Vegas
Henderson